ANTARCTICA

Go Exploring! Continents and Oceans

By Steffi Cavell-Clarke

©This edition was published in 2018. First published in 2017.

Book Life
King's Lynn
Norfolk PE30 4LS

ISBN: 978-1-78637-039-6

Written by:
Steffi Cavell-Clarke

Edited By:
Grace Jones

Designed by:
Drue Rintoul

A catalogue record for this book is available from the British Library.

ANTARCTICA

CONTENTS

Words in **red** can be found in the glossary on page 23.

WHAT IS A CONTINENT?

A continent is a very large area of land that covers part of the Earth's surface. There are seven continents in total. There are also five oceans that surround the seven continents.

ARCTIC OCEAN

EUROPE

ASIA

NORTH AMERICA

ATLANTIC OCEAN

AFRICA

SOUTH AMERICA

EQUATOR

INDIAN OCEAN

AUSTRALIA

PACIFIC OCEAN

SOUTHERN OCEAN

ANTARCTICA

The seven continents are home to the Earth's **population**. Each continent has many different types of weather, landscape and wildlife. Let's go exploring!

WHERE IS ANTARCTICA?

Planet Earth has two **polar regions**, which are the most northern and the most southern parts of the world. These are called the North Pole and the South Pole. The continent of Antarctica sits on the South Pole, the most southern part of the world.

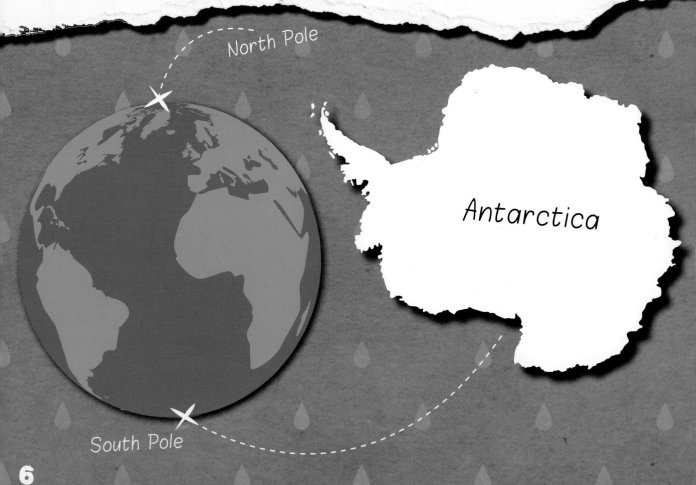

North Pole

South Pole

Antarctica

Antarctica is the coldest continent on Earth. It is completely covered by ice and is surrounded by the cold Southern Ocean.

Southern Ocean

Icy Antarctica

Antarctica is almost twice the size of Australia!

OCEANS

An ocean is an extremely large area of salt water. Oceans stretch along the coasts of the continents into wide, open waters. The Southern Ocean circles around Antarctica and flows into the Atlantic, Indian and Pacific Oceans.

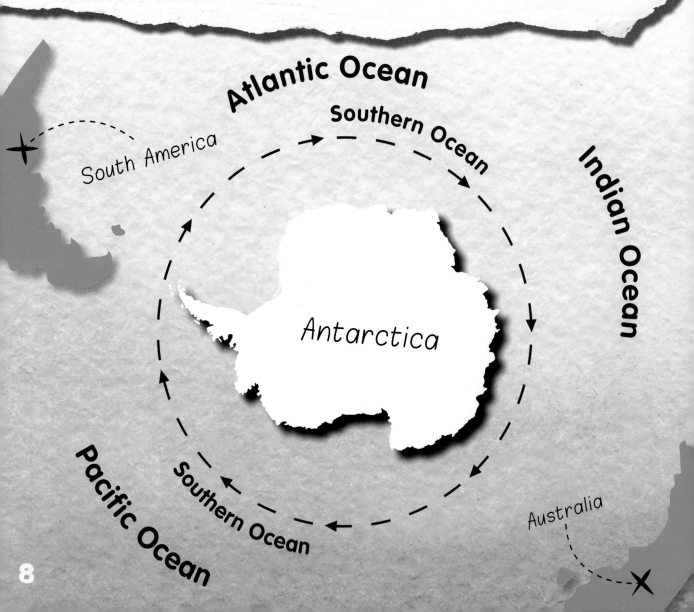

Atlantic Ocean

Southern Ocean

South America

Indian Ocean

Antarctica

Pacific Ocean

Southern Ocean

Australia

The weather around the Southern Ocean is very windy and it often has freezing temperatures. In the winter, nearly half of the Southern Ocean is covered in ice.

The winter months in Antarctica are June to September.

COUNTRIES

Unlike the other six continents, Antarctica doesn't have any countries. However, it does have **territories**, which are large areas of land claimed by other countries, such as France and the United Kingdom.

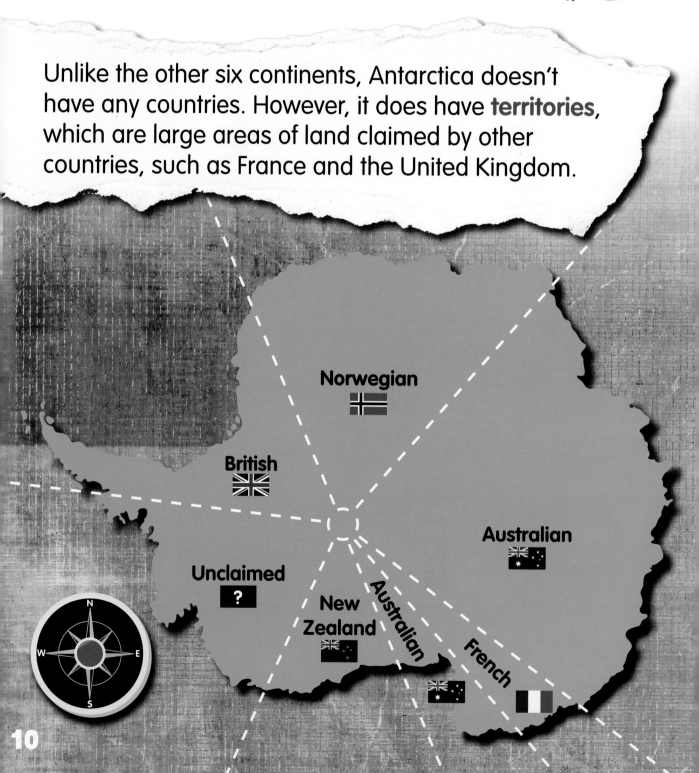

Norwegian

British

Australian

Unclaimed
?

New Zealand

Australian

French

In 1959, a **treaty** declared that Antarctica could only be used for science. Today, there are over 30 **research bases** where scientists work on the continent. Here, scientists can research things like the Earth's **climate**.

WEATHER

Antarctica has the most extreme weather on Earth. In the winter months, there is no daylight because the continent faces away from the Sun at this time of year. This is the coldest season of the year and the temperature can fall below -40°C.

Even though Antarctica is covered in snow and ice, it is actually considered to be the largest **desert** on earth because there is hardly any rainfall.

This is called a polar desert.

LANDSCAPE

Most of Antarctica is covered in a sheet of ice which can be several kilometres deep. This is called an ice cap.
In the winter, the ice grows to almost twice as large.
This is because the sea around the land freezes.

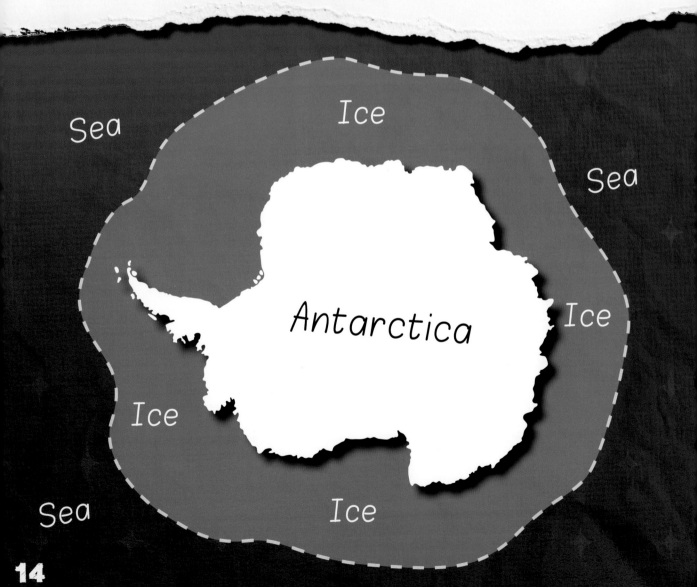

The ice that forms around the land is called an ice shelf. This thick sheet of ice floats on the ocean's surface, but is permanently attached to land. By the summer, the ice begins to melt again.

Sea ice melting in the summer months.

The landscape of Antarctica is very uneven, and there are many mountains and high peaks. Mount Vinson is the highest peak in Antarctica at 4,892 metres.

Mountains in Antarctica.

Sometimes large pieces of ice can break away from the ice shelf and float away in the ocean. These are called icebergs. There are many large icebergs floating in the Southern Ocean.

Floating iceberg in the Southern Ocean.

Almost 90% of an iceberg stays underwater, so only the tip is visible.

WILDLIFE

Antarctica is home to the emperor penguin. They are the biggest **species** of penguin and they can survive in Antarctica's harsh living conditions. They huddle together to keep warm in the coldest of weather.

1.2 metres

Penguins cannot fly, but they are great swimmers!

Seals can also be found in Antarctica. They have a layer of fat under their skin called **blubber**, which keeps them warm in the cold Antarctic waters.

VISITORS

There are not any human beings who permanently live in Antarctica, but it does have many visitors. Many **tourists** travel to Antarctica to see the wildlife and the beautiful, icy landscapes.

Everyone who visits Antarctica must have survival training because of the harsh and dangerous environment.

Many explorers have travelled to Antarctica to explore the landscape and wildlife and they hope to make many more new discoveries!

ROALD AMUNDSEN

2009

750F

RWANDA

The Norwegian explorer, Roald Amundsen, was the first man to reach the South Pole on the 14th December 1911.

THE ENVIRONMENT

The world's temperature is increasing due to human activity. This is called **global warming**. As the temperature rises, it begins to melt the ice sheets in Antarctica. This will raise the sea level and cause flooding all around the world.

GLOSSARY

blubber thick layer of fat under an animal's skin

climate the average weather of an area

desert areas of land that receive very little rainfall

global warming the slow rise of the earth's temperature

polar regions areas surrounding the North and South Poles

population number of people living in a place

research bases buildings for scientists to study in

species a type of animal

territories areas of land claimed by a country

tourists visitors from another place

treaty a formal agreement between countries

INDEX

PHOTOCREDITS